INSIDE THE
NFL

LOS ANGELES
CHARGERS

BY ROBERT COOPER

SportsZone

An Imprint of Abdo Publishing
abdobooks.com

abdobooks.com

Published by Abdo Publishing, a division of ABDO, PO Box 398166, Minneapolis, Minnesota 55439. Copyright © 2020 by Abdo Consulting Group, Inc. International copyrights reserved in all countries. No part of this book may be reproduced in any form without written permission from the publisher. SportsZone™ is a trademark and logo of Abdo Publishing.

Printed in the United States of America, North Mankato, Minnesota
042019
092019

Cover Photo: Peter Read Miller/AP Images
Interior Photos: Timothy A. Clary/AFP/Getty Images, 5; Jeff Haynes/AFP/Getty Images, 7; Keith Kracocic/AP Images, 9; Walter Iooss Jr./Set Number: X10469/Sports Illustrated/Getty Images, 11; NFL Photos/AP Images, 13, 14, 16, 21; Al Messerschmidt/AP Images, 18, 24; Chuck Solomon/AP Images, 23; AP Images, 27; Tom DiPace/AP Images, 29; G. Norman Lowrance/AP Images, 31; Phil Sandlin/AP Images, 33, 43; Matt A. Brown/Icon Sportswire/AP Images, 35; Greg Trott/AP Images, 36; Paul Spinelli/AP Images, 39; Kevin Terrell/AP Images, 41

Editor: Patrick Donnelly
Series Designer: Craig Hinton

Library of Congress Control Number: 2018965652

Library of Congress Cataloging-in-Publication Data

Names: Cooper, Robert, author.
Title: Los Angeles Chargers / by Robert Cooper
Description: Minneapolis, Minnesota: Abdo Publishing, 2020 | Series: Inside the NFL | Includes online resources and index.
Identifiers: ISBN 9781532118531 (lib. bdg.) | ISBN 9781532172717 (ebook)
Subjects: LCSH: Los Angeles Chargers (Football team)--Juvenile literature. | National Football League--Juvenile literature. | Football teams--Juvenile literature. | American football--Juvenile literature.
Classification: DDC 796.33264--dc23

TABLE OF CONTENTS

CHAPTER 1

LIGHTNING STRIKES IN PITTSBURGH

The Pittsburgh Steelers were three yards away from another trip to the Super Bowl. They were facing the San Diego Chargers in the American Football Conference (AFC) Championship Game in Pittsburgh on January 15, 1995.

The Steelers had been to the Super Bowl four times, winning them all. The Chargers were trying desperately to get there for the first time.

Steelers quarterback Neil O'Donnell had been picking apart San Diego's defense as he drove his team down the field in the game's final minute. Three more yards and the Steelers would be heading to Miami for the Super Bowl.

On fourth down, O'Donnell focused on running back Barry Foster. So did Chargers linebacker Dennis Gibson.

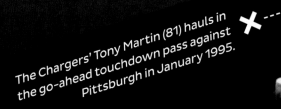

The Chargers' Tony Martin (81) hauls in the go-ahead touchdown pass against Pittsburgh in January 1995.

The rugged linebacker swooped in front of Foster and knocked O'Donnell's pass to the turf. The Chargers jumped for joy as they ran off the field, their arms upraised.

Three Rivers Stadium went from the verge of mayhem to shocked silence on a rainy Sunday afternoon. Somehow, some way, the underdog Chargers had done it. They had held on for a 17–13 win. It sent them to the Super Bowl after years of coming up short.

Getting to the Super Bowl was not easy for the Chargers. It would have been impossible if not for the play of tight end Alfred Pupunu and wide receiver Tony Martin against the Steelers. They each caught 43-yard touchdown passes, but the plays could not have been more different.

CLOSE CALL

The Chargers almost didn't make it to Pittsburgh to face the Steelers. A week earlier, they trailed the Miami Dolphins 21–6 at halftime of their first playoff game. San Diego started its comeback with a safety midway through the third quarter. Then Natrone Means ran for a touchdown to cut Miami's lead to 21–15. That remained the score until the final three minutes, when Stan Humphries marched the Chargers 61 yards in 10 plays. He capped the drive with an 8-yard touchdown pass to wide receiver Mark Seay. John Carney's extra point kick gave San Diego a 22–21 lead with 35 seconds to play. Miami had a chance to win, but a 48-yard field-goal attempt was no good and the Chargers held on.

Dennis Gibson celebrates the Chargers' victory over the Steelers in the AFC Championship Game in January 1995.

Pupunu's main job, usually, was to block in San Diego's running game. But in the third quarter he slipped downfield, and Chargers quarterback Stan Humphries spotted him wide open near the Steelers' 20-yard line. The 260-pound Pupunu caught the pass and rumbled down the sideline, beating

SEAU, SAY WOW

While Dennis Gibson made the key play in the AFC Championship Game against the Steelers, fellow linebacker Junior Seau had one of the greatest games of his career in helping the Chargers win. He almost single-handedly kept San Diego in the game in the first half, when its sputtering offense could provide only a field goal by John Carney. The Chargers were still in it, though, thanks to Seau's rib-rattling tackles. He finished with 16 that day.

Steelers safety Darren Perry to the end zone for a touchdown. That cut Pittsburgh's lead to 13–10.

In the fourth quarter, Humphries lofted a long pass toward Martin, who was a step ahead of his defender. Martin made a brilliant over-the-shoulder catch at the goal line and tumbled into the end zone. The touchdown gave San Diego the lead 17–13 with 5:13 to play.

When the team returned to San Diego after the AFC title game, it was met by an estimated crowd of 70,000 at Jack Murphy Stadium that night. The Chargers had won plenty of big games. But this one was the biggest.

The euphoria lasted just two weeks. The Chargers were routed 49–26 by the San Francisco 49ers in Super Bowl XXIX. It would prove to be the team's only appearance in the National Football League (NFL) championship game while in San Diego.

✕ The Chargers' Junior Seau, *right*, makes one of his 16 tackles in the AFC Championship Game in January 1995.

Although the Chargers could not keep the momentum going after the win in Pittsburgh, the team still held one league championship from much earlier. The Chargers were a power in the opening days of the American Football League (AFL), when they began play in the city they would abandon, only to return more than 50 years later.

CHAPTER 2

CALIFORNIA BORN AND RAISED

The Chargers are still building their future in Los Angeles. But the City of Angels is a part of their past, too. The team played its first season there in 1960 as one of the eight original members of the AFL, a league that started as a rival to the NFL. All eight are still in the NFL, though some have changed cities. The AFL featured a colorful style of play and equally colorful uniforms.

The Chargers' name was chosen because "Charge" was a favorite cheer at University of Southern California (USC) football games at the Los Angeles Memorial Coliseum. The Chargers' lightning bolt logo and blue and yellow team colors date to the team's beginning. In addition to USC, the Chargers shared the Coliseum with the Rams of the NFL.

Keith Lincoln (22) was one of the Chargers' first star players.

THE MURPH

One of the key figures in bringing the Chargers to San Diego was Jack Murphy. He was a columnist and sports editor at the *San Diego Union* newspaper.

Murphy would continue to have a big impact on the Chargers well beyond their move to San Diego in 1961. In the early 1960s, he began pushing for a new stadium. The idea was that the stadium could be the home to the Chargers and to the Major League Baseball team that Murphy was trying to attract. That new stadium opened in 1967. It was called San Diego Stadium.

In 1969 the San Diego Padres baseball team began playing in the stadium. It was renamed Jack Murphy Stadium after his death in 1980. It became known simply as "The Murph." Though the name changed in 1997 and again in 2017 due to corporate sponsorships, many San Diegans continue to call it "The Murph."

During the exhibition opener on August 6, 1960, at the Coliseum, Paul Lowe returned a kickoff 105 yards for a touchdown on the first play in team history. This helped the Chargers to a 27–7 victory over the New York Titans. The Chargers were a hit in their first regular-season game as well. They rallied to beat the Dallas Texans 21–20.

Overall it was a successful first season. The team leader was quarterback Jack Kemp. He would go on to become a congressman from New York and run for vice president of the United States in 1996. The Chargers finished with a record of

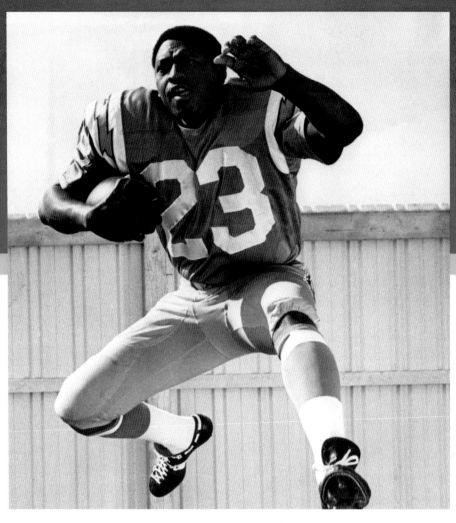

✕ Paul Lowe was a Charger from 1960 to 1968. He was a first-team all-AFL pick in 1965 when he led the league with 1,121 rushing yards.

10–4 to win the Western Division. They advanced to the AFL Championship Game but lost to the Houston Oilers 24–16.

Even as the Chargers were playing in that title game, team owner Barron Hilton had begun exploring a move to San Diego.

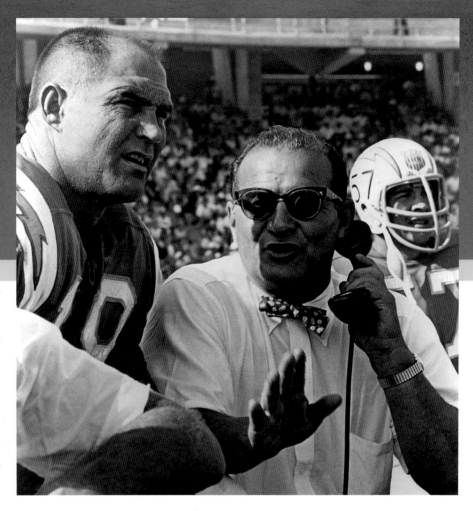

Chargers quarterback Tobin Rote, *left*, listens in as head coach Sid Gillman gives instructions to his team.

The Chargers seemed to be an afterthought in Los Angeles. They played in front of small crowds. San Diego was a quiet little navy town where civic officials were hungry for major league sports.

The AFL gave Hilton approval to move. The capacity at San Diego's Balboa Stadium was increased from 23,000 to 34,000. A new chapter in the city's sports history was beginning.

Although the NFL was the established big brother, the AFL had a personality all its own. The Chargers fit right in with the new league.

GILLMAN GETS IN

Sid Gillman was the Chargers' first coach and later their general manager. He was inducted into the Pro Football Hall of Fame in 1983. He was an innovator in the passing game and became the first coach to win division titles in both the NFL and the AFL. He had an overall record of 87–57–6 with the Chargers, including the playoffs.

The Chargers did not have the growing pains so often associated with new teams. The AFL attracted some great players, and the Chargers certainly had their share. Among them were quarterbacks Kemp, Tobin Rote, and John Hadl, wide receiver Lance Alworth, and running backs Lowe and Keith Lincoln.

Those players gave the Chargers an early identity and played high-scoring football. This thrilled the crowds that flocked to sun-splashed Balboa Stadium, located on the edge of downtown San Diego.

 Future Hall of Fame wide receiver Lance Alworth was a standout for San Diego from 1962 to 1970.

Lowe was speedy, and Lincoln was tough. They both could hit the hole and rip off huge chunks of yardage. The Chargers had quality quarterbacks in Kemp, Rote, and Hadl. Meanwhile, Alworth was so fast and graceful that he was nicknamed

"Bambi." It might not seem like the ideal nickname for a professional football player. But in his case, it fit.

The Chargers had 10 or more wins in three of their first four seasons. They won the Western Division championship in 1960 and 1961.

But the Chargers just could not get past quarterback George Blanda and the Houston Oilers in the AFL Championship Game. The Oilers won the first AFL title by beating the Chargers in Houston. The budding rivals met again for the AFL championship the next season. This time the game was played in San Diego. But the result was the same. Houston took the title with a 10–3 victory.

In 1963 it all came together for the Chargers. They won the Western Division with a record of 11–3 and got to host the AFL Championship Game at Balboa Stadium against the Boston Patriots. Lincoln responded with a remarkable game. He had

A MAN CALLED BAMBI

Lance Alworth remains one of the most popular Chargers ever, even decades after he caught his last pass for the team. He joined the team out of the University of Arkansas in 1962. He was nicknamed "Bambi" because of his graceful speed and ability to leap high to haul in passes. He was the epitome of the 1960s Chargers. San Diego traded Alworth to the Dallas Cowboys in 1971. In 1978 he became the first AFL player to be inducted into the Pro Football Hall of Fame.

✖ John Hadl was the Chargers' quarterback from 1962 to 1972.

349 total yards and two touchdowns in leading the Chargers to
a 51–10 victory. Lincoln was almost unstoppable that day. He
ran for 206 yards, including a 67-yard touchdown gallop that
is still shown on highlight reels. He caught seven passes for
123 yards and a touchdown. He even completed a 20-yard pass.

The Chargers continued to play winning football through the rest of the 1960s. After winning the championship in 1963, they made it back to the league's title contest each of the next two seasons. Both times they faced the Buffalo Bills and their old teammate, quarterback Jack Kemp. The Chargers, however, could not recapture the magic of 1963.

In the 1964 title contest, Lincoln was forced out of the game with a broken rib. Alworth already was out with an injury. Rote threw two interceptions, and Kemp sealed a 20–7 victory for host Buffalo with a 1-yard touchdown run.

The next year, the Chargers hosted the Bills in the title game. It was more of the same, though. Hadl was intercepted twice in a 23–0 Bills victory. Kemp threw a touchdown pass for Buffalo.

The Chargers didn't finish higher than third place in the division the rest of the decade, despite having a winning record each season. However, a new era was on the horizon. The Chargers, along with the rest of the AFL teams, were about to join the NFL.

CHAPTER 3

AIR CORYELL
TAKES OFF

The 1970s started out poorly for the Chargers. Instead of repeating the magic of the 1960s, they endured one of the worst periods in team history. They had records that made players and fans cringe, never earning more than six wins in a season.

However, one big move that would shape their future had already been made. Several more important moves would come later in the decade.

In what would turn out to be one of the most significant draft picks in team history, the Chargers selected quarterback Dan Fouts from the University of Oregon in the third round of the 1973 NFL Draft. The Chargers also acquired star quarterback Johnny Unitas from the Baltimore

The Chargers' Dan Fouts threw the ball often, and with great success, under head coach Don Coryell.

There is a pretty good reason the Air Coryell years were so good. Four players from those teams ended up being voted into the Pro Football Hall of Fame. Quarterback Dan Fouts, tight end Kellen Winslow, wide receiver Charlie Joiner, and defensive end Fred Dean all earned their Hall of Fame credentials during this era.

Colts that year. He played only one season with the Chargers before he retired.

Fouts was a hard-nosed, rugged competitor who was easily recognized by his bushy beard. He struggled along with the rest of the Chargers through the dismal years of the early to mid-1970s. He was winless in six starts as a rookie. He then went 3–8 in his second season. That is how it went for the next few seasons as the Chargers struggled to find their identity.

That identity would begin to be formed almost immediately after San Diego hired Don Coryell as head coach in September 1978. The Chargers had started that season with a 1–3 record. That led head coach Tommy Prothro to quit. San Diego fans were already familiar with Coryell. He had coached at San Diego State University from 1961 to 1972. The Chargers lost three of their first four games under Coryell. But then things began to click. They went 7–1 down the stretch to finish 9–7 in 1978. It was their first winning season since 1969.

✗ Don Coryell coached the Chargers from 1978 to 1986. He led them to the playoffs four times.

It also was the beginning of "Air Coryell." During this era, the high-flying Chargers redefined the passing game in the NFL. Coryell turned Fouts loose. Fouts responded with three straight seasons in which he passed for more than 4,000 yards.

✗ Chargers tight end Kellen Winslow is helped off the field after his extraordinary playoff effort against the Dolphins in January 1982.

At first Fouts relied heavily on wide receivers Charlie Joiner and John Jefferson. But in 1979 the Chargers made another innovation. They drafted tight end Kellen Winslow. He proved that tight ends do not always have to block. Winslow became one of the premier pass catchers in the NFL. He led the team in receptions for four straight years, from 1980 to 1983. He was fast and strong. Opponents simply could not figure out a way to stop him.

The Chargers went 12–4 in 1979 and reached the playoffs for the first time in 14 years. They suffered a disappointing 17–14 loss to the Houston Oilers in the divisional round. The Chargers went 11–5 and made the postseason again the next year. They earned some long-overdue revenge against the Buffalo Bills, beating them 20–14 in the divisional round.

That earned the Chargers a shot at the rival Oakland Raiders in the AFC Championship Game. With a trip to the Super Bowl at stake, the host Chargers fell behind by three touchdowns in the first half. They simply could not catch up. They lost 34–27.

The next season, the Chargers played in perhaps two of the most memorable playoff games in the history of pro football. The games were held in extreme conditions.

"SAN DIEGO SUPER CHARGERS"

Perhaps one of the catchiest fight songs of all time originated during the Air Coryell years. It is a disco song titled "San Diego Super Chargers." It was recorded in a Los Angeles studio in 1979 by R&B vocalist James Gaylen and released under the name "Captain Q. B. & the Big Boys." Despite its age, it was still played at Chargers games until the end of their time in San Diego.

INSTANT CLASSIC

San Diego's 41–38 overtime victory in the playoffs at Miami on January 2, 1982, remains one of the greatest games in NFL history. The Chargers jumped to a 24–0 lead in the first quarter. The Dolphins surged back to take the lead. Then the Chargers tied the score on Dan Fouts's 9-yard touchdown pass to James Brooks with 58 seconds left in regulation. Both teams missed field goals in overtime. Finally, after 13:52 had elapsed in the extra period, Rolf Benirschke kicked a 27-yard field goal to win it.

One of the lasting images of that game was the sight of exhausted tight end Kellen Winslow with a towel over his head, being helped off the field by two teammates. Despite cramping up in the extreme heat and humidity, Winslow caught 13 passes for 166 yards and one touchdown. He also blocked a potential game-winning field goal at the end of regulation.

The Chargers beat the Dolphins 41–38 in overtime in tropical Miami. The game could only be described as an epic struggle. The next week, however, the Chargers were completely out of their element. They traveled to frozen Cincinnati and lost 27–7 to the Bengals in the AFC Championship Game. Often referred to as the "Freezer Bowl," the game was played in the coldest wind-chill factor in NFL history. An air temperature of minus-9 degrees Fahrenheit (minus-23ºC) led to a wind chill of minus-38 (minus-39ºC) at kickoff. It's no wonder the Chargers froze up in a 27–7 loss.

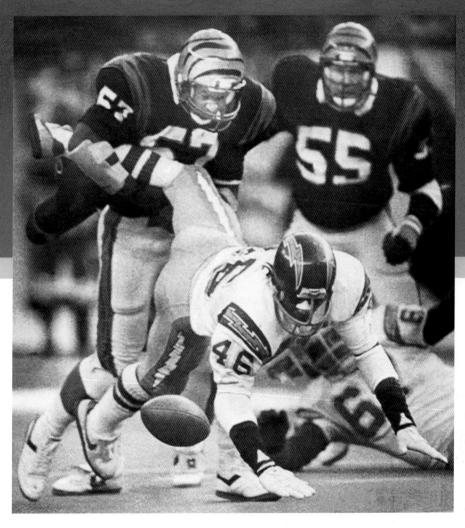

✕ Running back Chuck Muncie (46) coughs up the ball in frigid conditions as the Chargers lost to the Bengals in the AFC title game in January 1982.

The Chargers never did make it to the Super Bowl under Coryell. That fact often is lost in the pure excitement those years provided.

CHAPTER 4

SUPER BOWL SUPER CHARGERS

The Chargers had a frustrating habit of going into long slumps. It happened again in the 1980s. The Chargers returned to the playoffs in 1982. But then Air Coryell started coming back to earth. The playoff berths dried up. The era officially ended on October 29, 1986, when Don Coryell resigned as coach after a 1–7 start. It was a sad day in San Diego's sports history. Quarterback Dan Fouts retired after the 1987 season. He finally could not handle any more of the poundings he'd been absorbing.

Head coaches and starting quarterbacks would come and go. Losing seasons piled up. Then, just as earlier in team history, it took only one hire to start the process of turning the team around. On January 3, 1990, the Chargers

Junior Seau developed into one of the best linebackers in NFL history during his time with the Chargers.

SPANOS IN CHARGE

As of 2019, the Chargers were owned by the Spanos family. Real estate developer Alex Spanos purchased the team in 1984 and turned the day-to-day control of the club over to his son Dean in 1994. While Dean remains chairman, his sons, John and A. G., are more involved with the team's football operations. Dean was at the forefront of the team's failed efforts to build a new stadium in San Diego.

made Bobby Beathard their general manager. He had spent the previous decade building Washington into perennial champions. The team played in three Super Bowls and won two during the 1980s.

Beathard's first draft pick for the Chargers was a home run. He selected linebacker Junior Seau from the University of Southern California with the fifth pick overall in the 1990 NFL Draft. Seau had grown up in Oceanside, a suburb of San Diego. He brought an instant spark to the defense with his energetic play. Seau knew only one speed: full-speed ahead. He played the same way whether it was in practice or on Sundays.

The turnaround under Beathard took time. The Chargers were 6–10 and 4–12 in his first two seasons in charge. That led him to make another outstanding decision. He reached into the college ranks and hired coach Bobby Ross from Georgia Tech before the 1992 season. He also traded with Washington for quarterback Stan Humphries during training camp.

✕ Chargers quarterback Stan Humphries airs one out against Kansas City in 1994.

The Ross-Humphries era did not get off to a great start. The Chargers lost their first four games. They finished 11–5, however, and won the AFC West. They became the first team in NFL history to lose their first four games and still make the playoffs.

They returned to the postseason after a nine-year absence and defeated the division rival Kansas City Chiefs 17–0. To celebrate the victory, the team resurrected its disco-era song, "San Diego Super Chargers." The Bolts were back.

The Chargers went from one shutout to another. The next week, they lost 31–0 in the rain at Miami. It was a disappointing end to a remarkable season. But Chargers fans embraced the feeling of a winning record and a return to the playoffs.

Two years later, the Chargers put it all together. They finished 11–5, won the AFC West title, and earned a bye in the first round of the playoffs. They rallied to beat visiting Miami 22–21 in their postseason opener. They then stunned the Steelers 17–13 in Pittsburgh to advance to the Super Bowl for the first time. It was an all-California final: the Chargers against the San Francisco 49ers.

San Diego had Super Bowl fever. While few people outside the city thought the Chargers could win, the team's fans were confident. Unfortunately for the Chargers, they were overwhelmed in one of the biggest blowouts in Super Bowl history. They allowed a Super Bowl-record six touchdown passes by 49ers quarterback Steve Young and were routed 49–26.

Despite the blowout, the Chargers were welcomed back the next day with a parade through downtown San Diego. The shock was still fresh. But fans wanted to celebrate a breakthrough season.

✗ Andre Coleman returns a kickoff 98 yards for a touchdown against the 49ers, one of the Chargers' few bright spots in their Super Bowl loss.

Behind the scenes, the relationship between Beathard and Ross was falling apart. On January 3, 1997, Ross resigned and his staff was fired. Humphries suffered a concussion midway through the 1997 season, which ended with eight straight losses.

With a resulting high draft pick, the Chargers chose quarterback Ryan Leaf one pick after the Indianapolis Colts had selected Peyton Manning. Leaf was a disaster on and off the field, and the team hit rock bottom with a 1–15 season in 2000. Though only five years in the past, the team's Super Bowl appearance seemed like a distant memory.

CHAPTER 5

BIG LOSSES LEAD
BACK TO LA

That embarrassing 2000 season led owner Alex Spanos to hire a new general manager. John Butler was not afraid to take chances. His biggest was to trade the first overall pick in the 2001 NFL Draft to the Atlanta Falcons for a package of draft picks and players.

With the number five pick, the Chargers selected Texas Christian University running back LaDainian Tomlinson. It's hard to fathom it now, but there were some Chargers fans who were not happy. They wanted quarterback Michael Vick, whom Atlanta selected. The player San Diego got, however, turned out to be one of the top running backs in NFL history.

Tomlinson began establishing himself as a star from his first game, when he rushed for 113 yards and two

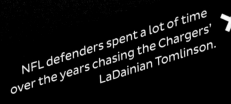

NFL defenders spent a lot of time over the years chasing the Chargers' LaDainian Tomlinson.

✖ Philip Rivers took over as the Chargers' starting quarterback in 2006.

touchdowns against Washington. The rebuilding process took a few years under coach Marty Schottenheimer. By 2004, though, the Chargers had returned to the playoffs.

Tomlinson was the runaway pick as the NFL's Most Valuable Player (MVP) in 2006 after scoring 31 touchdowns. He was the first Chargers player to receive the league's ultimate individual honor. Although he was clearly the star, the Chargers were slowly but surely building one of the most talented teams in the NFL. Among the other stars were quarterback Philip Rivers, tight end Antonio Gates, wide receiver Vincent Jackson, and outside linebacker Shawne Merriman.

With that talented roster, the Chargers enjoyed a lot of regular-season success. The team won five AFC West titles from 2004 to 2009. But the playoffs were a different story. The Chargers were haunted by heartbreaking defeats. Kicker Nate Kaeding missed a field goal that would have beaten the Jets after the 2004 season. Defensive back Marlon McCree dropped an interception that could have ended a divisional round game against the New England Patriots in January 2007. The Chargers seemed cursed.

The furthest San Diego advanced during that time was the AFC Championship Game in January 2008 under first-year head

ANTONIO GATES

Antonio Gates first rose to prominence as a college basketball player. He helped lead Kent State University within one win of the Final Four in 2002. Knowing that he probably had a better chance of playing tight end in the NFL than going to the National Basketball Association, he signed with the Chargers as a rookie free agent in 2003. Opposing defenses almost immediately found him hard to cover because of his size and leaping ability. He was the team's leading receiver every season from 2004 to 2009. In 2017 he broke the all-time record for touchdowns by a tight end with his 112th career score.

THE BIG TRADE

A few days before the 2004 NFL Draft, Archie Manning, a former quarterback in the league, asked the Chargers not to pick his son Eli with the number one selection.

The Chargers were coming off a 4–12 season. The Manning family apparently felt it was not a good situation for Eli, the younger brother of Colts star quarterback Peyton Manning.

Chargers general manager A. J. Smith picked Manning anyway. Smith then made one of the biggest trades in team history. He sent Manning to the New York Giants for the rights to quarterback Philip Rivers, a third-round choice that the Chargers used to select kicker Nate Kaeding, a 2005 first-round pick that the team used to select outside linebacker Shawne Merriman, and a 2005 fifth-round pick that San Diego traded to Tampa Bay for offensive tackle Roman Oben.

coach Norv Turner. Rivers was effective, despite playing with a torn knee ligament, but Tomlinson missed most of the game due to injury, and the Chargers lost 21–12 at New England.

Rivers was known for his toughness and fiery attitude throughout his career. He and Gates formed an incredible partnership. Through the end of the 2018 season, they had connected for 89 touchdowns. Along with Tomlinson, they formed a core that kept the Chargers competitive throughout the 2000s.

✖ Antonio Gates became a record-setting tight end with the Chargers.

Injuries and age took their toll on Tomlinson, though. The Chargers released him after their 2009 season ended with another playoff loss to the Jets. Tomlinson wound up joining the Jets in March 2010.

Turner was fired after a 7–9 season in 2012. New coach Mike McCoy led the Chargers back to the playoffs after the 2013 season. After beating the Bengals, they lost on the road to the Denver Broncos. By 2015 the team had fallen to 4–12 and dead last in the AFC West.

Off the field, the team faced uncertainty. For years team chairman Dean Spanos had asked San Diego for help in building a new stadium. But city officials and the team could never come to an agreement on the public's financial contribution or a suitable site for the stadium.

After the St. Louis Rams moved back to Los Angeles in 2016, the Chargers were given the option to join them and share a new stadium. Spanos decided to leave the team's home of 56 years. For the 2017 season, the Chargers relocated to Carson, California, at the StubHub Center. The stadium was a temporary home while the new stadium was being built in Inglewood.

The first season was tough on the Chargers and new head coach Anthony Lynn. They started out 0–4 before winning six of their last seven games and just missing the playoffs. But 2018 was a different story. Rivers threw 32 touchdown passes—10 of them to wide receiver Mike Williams. Fellow wideout Keenan Allen caught 97 passes for 1,196 yards. And a top-10 defense

LT'S RECORDS

LaDainian Tomlinson owns or shares 28 team records. During his nine seasons in San Diego, Tomlinson won two NFL rushing titles and set NFL single-season records with 28 rushing touchdowns and 31 total touchdowns in 2006. Tomlinson also set the NFL mark for most consecutive games with a rushing touchdown with 18. He left the Chargers after the 2009 season with 12,490 rushing yards. That was the eighth-best total in NFL history at that point.

The Chargers drafted running back Melvin Gordon in the first round in 2015. He was their leading rusher in each of the next four seasons.

helped keep opponents in check. It added up to a 12–4 season, followed by a playoff win at Baltimore.

With Rivers still under center, running back Melvin Gordon making Pro Bowls, defensive end Joey Bosa terrorizing quarterbacks, and Lynn calling the shots, the Chargers had hope of making it work in Los Angeles. Recent history showed they had a great chance to make it work.

TIMELINE

San Diego Stadium is dedicated on August 20 before an exhibition loss to the Detroit Lions, the Chargers' first game against an NFL team.

Keith Lincoln accounts for 349 total yards as the Chargers win the AFL Championship Game 51–10 against the Boston Patriots on January 5.

The Chargers beat the Oakland Raiders 44–0 on September 17 in the first regular-season game in San Diego.

The Chargers play the first regular-season game in franchise history, beating the visiting Dallas Texans 21–20 on September 10.

The Chargers receive permission from the AFL on February 10 to move to San Diego from Los Angeles.

1960

1961

1961

1964

1967

On January 23, former Chargers wide receiver Lance Alworth becomes the first player from the AFL to be elected to the Pro Football Hall of Fame.

San Diego Mayor Pete Wilson announces on December 22 that San Diego Stadium will be renamed Jack Murphy Stadium.

Rolf Benirschke's 29-yard field goal in overtime lifts the Chargers to an epic 41–38 playoff win over the host Miami Dolphins on January 2.

Quarterback Dan Fouts retires on March 24 after a 15-year career in which he passed for 43,040 yards.

The Chargers play in their first Super Bowl, losing to the San Francisco 49ers 49–26 on January 29.

1978

1980

1982

1988

1995

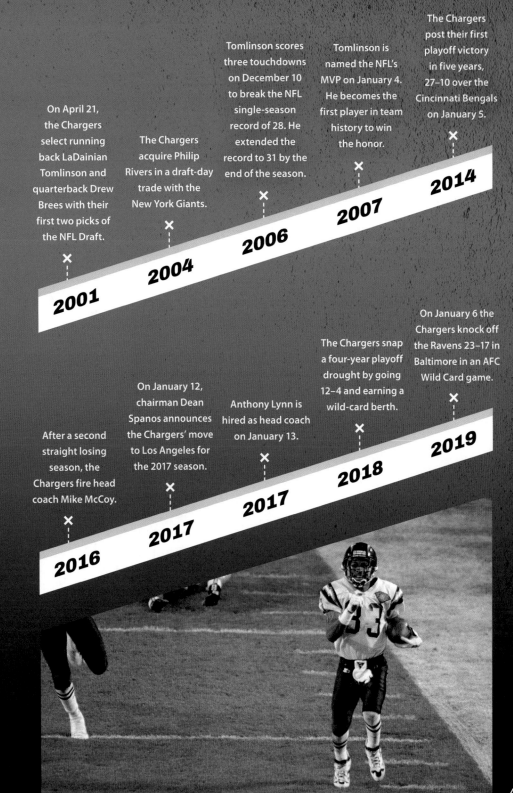

On April 21, the Chargers select running back LaDainian Tomlinson and quarterback Drew Brees with their first two picks of the NFL Draft.

The Chargers acquire Philip Rivers in a draft-day trade with the New York Giants.

Tomlinson scores three touchdowns on December 10 to break the NFL single-season record of 28. He extended the record to 31 by the end of the season.

Tomlinson is named the NFL's MVP on January 4. He becomes the first player in team history to win the honor.

The Chargers post their first playoff victory in five years, 27–10 over the Cincinnati Bengals on January 5.

2001

2004

2006

2007

2014

After a second straight losing season, the Chargers fire head coach Mike McCoy.

On January 12, chairman Dean Spanos announces the Chargers' move to Los Angeles for the 2017 season.

Anthony Lynn is hired as head coach on January 13.

The Chargers snap a four-year playoff drought by going 12–4 and earning a wild-card berth.

On January 6 the Chargers knock off the Ravens 23–17 in Baltimore in an AFC Wild Card game.

2016

2017

2017

2018

2019

QUICK STATS

FRANCHISE HISTORY

Los Angeles Chargers
(1960, 2017–)
San Diego Chargers (1961–2016)

SUPER BOWLS

1994 (XXIX)

AFL CHAMPIONSHIP GAMES *(1960–69, wins in bold)*

1960, 1961, **1963**, 1964, 1965

AFC CHAMPIONSHIP GAMES *(since 1970 AFL-NFL merger)*

1980, 1981, 1994, 2007

DIVISION CHAMPIONSHIPS *(since 1970 AFL-NFL merger)*

1979, 1980, 1981, 1992, 1994, 2004, 2006, 2007, 2008, 2009

KEY COACHES

Don Coryell (1978–86):
69–56, 3–4 (playoffs)
Sid Gillman (1960–69, 1971):
86–53–6, 1–4 (playoffs)
Bobby Ross (1992–96):
47–33, 3–3 (playoffs)

KEY PLAYERS *(positions, seasons with team)*

Lance Alworth (WR, 1962–70)
Fred Dean (DE, 1975–81)
Dan Fouts (QB, 1973–87)
Antonio Gates (TE, 2003–)
Melvin Gordon (RB, 2015–)
John Hadl (QB, 1962–72)
Charlie Joiner (WR, 1976–86)
Keith Lincoln (RB, 1961–66, 1968)
Ron Mix (OT, 1960–69)
Philip Rivers (QB, 2004–)
Junior Seau (LB, 1990–2002)
LaDainian Tomlinson (RB, 2001–09)
Eric Weddle (S, 2007–15)
Kellen Winslow (TE, 1979–87)

HOME FIELDS

StubHub Center (2017–)
Qualcomm Stadium (1967–2016)
Also known as Jack Murphy Stadium and San Diego Stadium
Balboa Stadium (1961–66)
Los Angeles Memorial Coliseum (1960)

*All statistics through 2018 season

QUOTES AND ANECDOTES

"After 15 years, this body has taken about as many hits as it can."

—Quarterback Dan Fouts, in announcing his retirement on March 24, 1988

"They thought this was only a tourist attraction. They know about Shamu. Now the world is going to know, not about Junior Seau, not about Natrone Means, not about Stan Humphries, not about Leslie O'Neal, but about the San Diego Chargers."

—Linebacker Junior Seau, to the estimated 70,000 fans who packed Jack Murphy Stadium to welcome home the Chargers after they upset the Pittsburgh Steelers in the AFC Championship Game on January 15, 1995

"This gets us out of the history books."

—Coach Mike Riley, after the Chargers beat the Kansas City Chiefs 17–16 on November 26, 2000, to improve to 1–11 and avoid potentially going 0–16.

"The Philip Rivers that San Diego's gotten over the last 13 years, that's what they're going to get up there. And I'm going to embrace that. And go like crazy. I'm not going to be there 13 years but I'm going to give them all I got for the short time I got left."

—Quarterback Philip Rivers on moving to Los Angeles in 2017

GLOSSARY

concussion
An injury to the brain usually sustained when a football player's head is slammed to the turf.

draft
The process by which teams select players who are new to the league.

exhibition
A game, typically played before the official start of the season, that does not factor into the standings.

franchise
An entire sports organization, including the players, coaches, and staff.

general manager
The executive who is in charge of the team's overall operation. He or she hires and fires coaches, drafts college players, and signs free agents.

legendary
Well known and admired over a long period.

retire
To end one's career.

rival
An opponent with whom a player or team has a fierce and ongoing competition.

rookie
A first-year player.

tight end
The player who lines up to the outside of the offensive tackle. He often blocks for the running back but can also catch passes.

MORE
INFORMATION

BOOKS

Cohn, Nate. *Los Angeles Chargers*. New York: AV2 by Weigl, 2018.

Graves, Will. *The Best NFL Offenses of All Time*. Minneapolis, MN: Abdo Publishing, 2014.

Kortemeier, Todd. *San Diego Chargers*. Minneapolis, MN: Abdo Publishing, 2017.

ONLINE RESOURCES

To learn more about the Los Angeles Chargers, visit **abdobooklinks.com** or scan this QR code. These links are routinely monitored and updated to provide the most current information available.

PLACE TO VISIT

Pro Football Hall of Fame
2121 George Halas Dr. NW
Canton, OH 44708
330–456–8207
profootballhof.com

This hall of fame and museum highlights the greatest players and moments in the history of the AFL and NFL. Among the Chargers enshrined are Lance Alworth, Dan Fouts, Junior Seau, and LaDainian Tomlinson.

INDEX

ABOUT THE AUTHOR

Robert Cooper is a retired law enforcement officer and lifelong NFL fan. He and his wife live in Seattle near their only son and two grandchildren